Lessons I had to Learn

CONSTANCE D. DARBY

ISBN 978-0-6921-7574-3
1. Motivational & Inspirational. 2. Personal Growth. I. Title.

Author's photography by Senae Photography

Printed in the United States of America

This book is dedicated to my late great-grandmother,

Josie Daniels Shelby, who for ninety-nine years

taught us Lessons to LIVE by.

CONTENTS

Introduction
Becoming a Butterfly

I woke up after a good night's rest and realized it was trash day. I didn't have much trash to take to the curb, but I did have items that needed to be recycled: water bottles, cans, boxes—useless objects that accumulate over time. I put on my robe, gathered my contributions to a greener earth, and carried them outside. Just as I dropped my big green bin next to the curb, out of the corner of my eye, I noticed it: a beautiful yellow and black butterfly. I couldn't remember the last time I'd seen a butterfly that close, but I had to capture that moment. Quickly coming to myself, I ran back into the house to grab my cell phone, all the while thinking, "I hope it's still there. I want to capture the moment." When I returned, it was in the exact spot, unmoved and unbothered. For a second, I thought it was dead, but then, much to my relief, it fluttered ever so slightly. It was still very much alive.

At that moment, I was reminded of a familiar yet relevant lesson. Traditionally, it's believed that the butterfly is a symbol of change and transformation. It represents newness, a new beginning. That morning I saw the butterfly's beauty and splendor. What I didn't see was the ever-changing process in the life of this butterfly. I didn't see the distinct *lessons* that transpired with each new season for the beautiful insect. I didn't see the butterfly's metamorphosis.

At one time, before our encounter that morning, that beautiful butterfly was just a caterpillar absorbing and indulging in everything needed for its next season of life. I could relate to this particular stage. The caterpillar's main task at this point is consumption. I've gained vital knowledge and learned purposeful lessons from experiences in my life. Many were good; some were not so good. But they are mine, and I own them! I've grown, processed my experiences, and essentially prepared myself for each subsequent season in my own life. And I definitely can appreciate those particular seasons of consuming all I can to prepare me for my future: Learn! Take on new tasks! Challenge myself! Grow!

Although we all experience stages of growth and maturity, each person's looks different. No two butterflies look the same, and no story is identical to another's. My story is mine. Your story is yours. Without gaining the knowledge of certain lessons at the appropriate time, my story would not be as God intended and I would not become who He called me to be. I simply would not have the capacity to stand in my purpose. He intended and orchestrated every experience in my life. Had I not learned to live as a "caterpillar," I would still be existing as an egg when, ultimately, I was called to be a butterfly. Or I could be stuck in this caterpillar stage when I needed to experience two more stages of growth and living. I had to learn essential lessons. I had to go through each process, regardless of their difficulty or how much I wanted to rush through them.

The caterpillar experiences growth in this stage, but, interestingly enough, the skin, or more accurately the exoskeleton, does not stretch to accommodate the insect's physical growth. Therefore, the caterpillar must shed its outgrown skin several times, which is paramount for growth. This is one of those uncomfortable but necessary lessons. Sometimes it's difficult for us to let go of the familiar to experience the better. Letting go of that which is no longer a part of your destiny can be uncomfortable. But shedding is necessary for growth. I learned that I had to sever ties for the proper change to take place in my life. God causes strategic separation because sometimes people are connected to us who were never meant to be there. The Bible says, "They went out from us, but they did not really belong to us. For if they had belonged to us, they would have remained with us; but their going showed that none of them belonged to us" (1 John 2:19).

How I viewed this "larval" stage of my life was completely up to me. I could see it as horrible and uncomfortable, or I could view it as a time of immense excitement and growth that allowed God to mold and shape me.

Though this stage of learning and growth is vital, it doesn't last long in the life cycle of the butterfly. The third stage, pupa, soon commences. The caterpillar goes to work and spins a protective chrysalis around itself to do what so many of us have had to learn, myself included: rest. Full of its food and nutrients, the caterpillar is now in a state of peaceful rest. To the naked eye, nothing else is going on. However, on the inside, a transformation is taking place, hidden and unseen. The body of the caterpillar is slowly dissolving, and the soon-to-emerge butterfly gradually develops into a brand-new being. The same stage is at work in our lives.

Recently at church, the pastor compelled us to rest, saying, "To God, rest is just as important as work." To be honest and transparent, I usually don't recognize the need for rest. I lived out the holy fallacy "busyness is next to godliness." It's a fallacy because it's so not true! I have kept busy in my career and my business. I've worked to serve and empower others in business and formed my own ministry to minister to other young ladies. My life can be pretty hectic. Many times, I don't recognize that I need to stop and take a break. This is especially true when I have a goal, dream, or arduous task at hand. However, we all need rest. I'm not talking about a nap in the middle of the day, but a true rest in God.

Learning to rest in God has been an amazing lesson because in resting, I'm conceding to His perfect will and plan. There have been times when I have had to stop laboring and stop striving and rest. It's a good place to be, as God welcomes us when we find rest in Him. Come to me all who labor . . . and I will give you rest. (Matt. 11:28 ESV). The pupa had to stop laboring and rest for a season, and so do we.

Now the final stage. It's in this last stage into which the butterfly emerges from its state of rest and breaks free. Its wings that were once bound are now able to take flight and share its beauty with the world. In this stage, I'm able to reflect on amazing moments in my life and lessons learned. I celebrate my metamorphosis and enjoy the moment, basking in the freedom I was created for.

This book culminates lessons I've learned through various stages and seasons of my life. Many of these lessons were birthed from pain, frustration, and agony. Others came from times when I trusted God to navigate my life. Like that butterfly in front of my house on that early Wednesday morning had to experience various stages in its life to become all it was meant to be, so are these *Lessons I Had to Learn.*

Lesson One
Live Unapologetically

I'm learning that life is so much better when you stop being who people want you to be . . . and be who God called you to be.

Dickson Guillaume

I praise you because I am fearfully and wonderfully made;
your works are wonderful,
I know that full well.
My frame was not hidden from you
when I was made in the secret place,
when I was woven together in the depths of the earth.
Your eyes saw my unformed body;
all the days ordained for me were written in your book
before one of them came to be.

Psalm 139:14–16

A lesson I had to learn is to be content with the woman God created me to be.

For as long as I can remember, I've felt different from my peers and friends. I loved going to church and being there all day. It was never burdensome for me. My parents would go home after morning worship on Sundays, but I would stay at church for evening services with my aunt. I loved church that much. Many times, we would eat between services with some of the other members of the church, most of whom were old enough to be my grandparents. Our age difference never bothered me.

I was different regarding school as well. I enjoyed attending school and learning. I didn't necessarily look forward to breaks because I liked my school and its environment. While most students counted down the days to the holiday or summer breaks, I was focused on getting the highest grade and excelling in my classes. I vividly remember when I got my first B on a report card. I was in the third grade. To me, I felt like I'd failed the entire class. I cried inconsolably and couldn't understand why this was happening to me! Never mind that my overall grade for the class was still an A. I was upset, and I let my teacher know, too.

I've been different for as long as I can remember. Why was I different? Why didn't I fit in? Did I have to be peculiar? And what did that mean to a young five-year-old? Or a sixteen-year-old in high school when everyone is trying "new" things? Or a twenty-one-year-old college student? Or a thirty-year-old young woman? It meant being confident in who God created me to be, unapologetically.

Once I embraced who I was, I owned it! I began to exude confidence in every area of my life. I understood my worth and my value. I understood that I am a daughter of the King. I realized that I'm royalty, so I picked up my diamond tiara and fixed it just right on my head, securing the combs in place with my coarse red hair. As I began to live my life unapologetically, I made a new discovery: although I was comfortable with who I was, it seemed my confidence threatened other people.

My mom tells the story of my experience as a little girl in kindergarten. I have to accept her account because I honestly don't remember the incident. However, at the young age of five, I'd already exemplified this confidence, which seemed to be a threat to my teacher. Though we were decades apart, something about me, she could not accept. Perhaps it was because I didn't try to be the teacher's pet. I knew who I was at five and was confident in myself. As a result of my confidence and independence, the teacher mistreated me. I was picked on and ostracized. I told my mother how I was treated at school and that the teacher didn't like me.

She didn't dislike me because I didn't do well in my academics. It wasn't because my conduct or attitude was disrespectful; rather, it was because she didn't understand the confidence I possessed. So my mom, being the mom that she is, was not going to allow this teacher to dim the light of her confident little girl. She met with my "threatened" teacher. I don't know what they discussed, but after the parent-teacher conversation, I was no longer picked on and ostracized.

In several instances my confidence has intimidated someone else: peers, adults, church members, classmates, men, and women. Rather than allow them to make me withdraw or become subdued, I lived unapologetically. I realized at a young age that everyone isn't going to like me. It's not their job to like me; it's mine. As long as I wasn't offending anyone or causing anyone to stumble, I had to live my life the best way I knew how: unapologetically.

Living with complete confidence and knowing who you are is liberating and rejuvenating. You're not bound to someone else's thoughts or opinions. Often, people allow others' perception to dictate how they live their lives. Most people have lived their entire lives this way. As babies, naturally, their parents' perceptions mold their lives. As students, their teachers' perceptions impact their lives. In college, their peers' perceptions influence their lives. Then as adults, society's perceptions govern their lives. They've gone through life living for someone else and not truly knowing who they are.

Know Who You Are

Oftentimes, we associate people with what they've accomplished or where they're from or who their families are. When you hear the name Michael Jordan, you immediately think of him as one of the greatest basketball players of all time. When you hear the name Beyoncé, some fans go crazy while others think of an amazing vocalist/entertainer who has become known as Queen Bey. When you hear Oprah, a great talk show host comes to mind. See? When we think of these people, we think of their accomplishments. We think of their awards and accolades or their status in our current culture. But the question remains, who are they? And because we don't know them personally, we can't know their essence or identity or personality. Though we see and read articles and hear gossip in the media, some things we will never know unless we develop a relationship with them.

To know who you are, you must have an understanding of your Maker. You received your DNA and physical characteristics from your parents, but the essence of who you are goes much deeper. God spoke to Jeremiah and said, "Before I formed you in the womb I knew you" (Jer. 1:5). It is the same for us. God designed a plan and purpose for each of us before we were born, before we were conceived, and even before we were a thought.

I've known who I am for a long time. Although it may not have been in kindergarten, I identified my purpose early on. It is comprised of my gifts and passions. It includes my personal values and beliefs. It encompasses who I want people to see when they look at me. I'm a leader and have been for a long time. I like leading people, and I'm not afraid to be in the front. While some people may shrink at opportunities to lead, I embrace them. It's my purpose!

In looking at different areas of my life, I've had several opportunities not only to lead but to influence others. I'm the oldest of my sisters, so I'm always leading even when I'm unaware. In high school, I was president of my church's Youth Ministry. I loved conducting our meetings and gatherings with my peers. The successes of our ministry gave me joy and a sense of accomplishment. As a senior in college, I was on the Executive Board of four organizations, three of which I served as president. As a business owner, I led people 24/7 in various capacities.

In 2011, I discovered my purpose: speaking about and ministering God's Word. That year was particularly difficult for me. I was on a relationship roller coaster. I was in a dark, dry place and had no idea that my purpose would be birthed there.

Regardless of this desert season, I mustered enough strength and courage to accept an invitation as the keynote speaker at a High School Baccalaureate church service. I prepared my speech on the topic I'd been given. I wasn't nervous on the day of the event, just excited to share with the graduates. As I was addressing the audience, a confirmation blossomed within me, and I knew that ministering and sharing God's Word with others was my purpose. I'd sung at church, directed the choir, coordinated events, and worked in corporate America, but none of those made me feel like this is why I was created.

I realized who I was and who God called me to be. It's not based on what I've done, but the essence of who I am. I have many accomplishments to my name: attended Sam Houston State University, joined Alpha Kappa Alpha Sorority, Incorporated. I am a Certified Public Accountant in the state of Texas and a business owner. I teach in our church's Women's class and host a home Bible study for women. However, those undertakings are my accolades, my responsibilities. But they are not who I am. If you aren't careful, people will associate who you are by what you do, even the wrong you've done.

A Purpose Bigger than Her Past

Though she had developed into an intelligent woman and was aware of the past victories of Israel, even while it was preparing to besiege her own country, Rahab's past always followed her. While she exemplified initiative in hiding the Hebrew spies and arranging the deliverance of her entire family, whenever her name appears in the Scriptures, you see what she did, not who she was. She became the mother of Boaz and was essential to the lineage of King David and Jesus. Nevertheless, Rahab was always known as the harlot. Scripture mentions her several times by what she'd done (Matt. 1:5; Heb. 11:31; James 2:25), yet her constant reoccurrence in Scripture is actually attributed to who she was and her contribution to God's divine plan. She was discerning, intelligent, and possessed spiritual insight. Her identity was not relegated to her past, but a choice she made when she became aware of God's reality.

Rahab demonstrated her true identity when she successfully hid the Jewish spies that had come to survey the land behind the walls of Jericho. She allowed the men to seek cover in her home to avoid being found by the guards who suspected their entrance into the city. When speaking to the two men, she said that she knew they were Israeli spies and that their people were planning to attack Jericho. She was possibly more aware and confident of God's intervention for the people of Israel than the Israelites themselves.

The guards came to Rahab's house, seeking the spies. After all, most men stopped by her house while they were in the city because she was a known harlot. But Rahab knew she had a purpose bigger than her past. So she diverted the guards. When they had gone a distance away, Rahab obtained from the spies a promise of protection for her and her entire family during the Israelite's attack. She fastened a scarlet rope on her window, and when the Israelites came to siege the land, they did not touch her or those in her household. She had a past, but her identity was measured by her faith. It didn't matter what she'd done, Rahab's courageous acts showed who she really was: a discerning deliverer of her people.

Embrace Your Flaws

I love that Rahab didn't let her flaws hinder her from being a deliverer. Her purpose was bigger than her flaws, and because she knew her purpose, her flaws were diminished.

It is possible that your purpose can be birthed in a flawed place. But God has a way of calling the flawed faithful. We all have flaws—thinking, attitudes, and actions that aren't ideal, that we regret or wish were different. Nevertheless, don't focus on the flaw; focus on the strengths. For instance, if you're assertive and strong-willed, focus on your ability to lead and accomplish tasks effectively. If you're a people person and love being around others, focus on how you have a way of brightening someone's day and encouraging others when they're down. The more we magnify our strengths, the smaller our flaws become. Most people, on the contrary, focus so much attention on their flaws and shortcomings that they ignore their strengths. So rather than focus on those matters in life that might be perceived as negatives, welcome the passions you possess. It's that passion that fuels who you are, and you should embrace it.

Our society has overextended the pendulum of identifying our flaws. In an attempt to avoid arrogance or conceit, we sometimes magnify our flaws and never shed light on the strengths we possess. So when someone offers us a compliment, we divert the attention from the praise by negating it. For example, if someone compliments you, you say, "Oh, I've had this dress for years," or "I don't think I did that well," or "It could have been better." We tend to shun any attention that brings praise or recognition while highlighting our flaws. In the process, our strengths are overshadowed.

When identifying your flaws, be very cautious. In many situations, people have tried to project their insecurities on me and call that my flaw. Maybe they fall short in a certain area, or maybe I don't conform to how they think I should be (their expectations), and then they call me flawed. The sooner I identified what they were doing; the easier life was for me. Because it can be easy to succumb to who people think I am or try to fit into a box they created for me, it is vital for me to know who I am.

My flaws are a part of me, but they aren't the essence of me. I've embraced them, but they do not make me who I am. Because I know that everyone has flaws, I'm not too hard on myself; rather, I identify them and know that when I work on them and address them, they eventually will go away. I'll own them unapologetically, but I won't make them larger than they are. This is liberating.

It's okay that I'm different and don't fit in. It's okay that I don't do things the way other people do them. I don't have to be perfect. I'm a work in progress, but I know exactly who I am, and who I'm called to be—flaws and all. I can be me and live unapologetically. You can too!

Lesson Two
Live for One

You are second to none. You are daughters of God.

Gordon B. Hinckley

You turned my wailing into dancing;
you removed my sackcloth and clothed me with joy,
that my heart may sing your praises and not be silent.
Lord my God, I will praise you forever.

Psalm 30:11–12

A lesson I had to learn is that I am not called to please everyone.

It sounds like an easy concept for a confident person, and really it should be, but it was a hard-won lesson I struggled to learn. (Well, it's something I still occasionally wrestle with, but now I've identified it as a flaw.) I wasn't intentionally trying to please people; it just manifested in my actions and interactions. I wanted people to accept my confidence. I wanted to be liked. I wanted to fit in. As a result, I tried to please others—friends, family, and guys with whom I was in relationship. All of my efforts failed.

In high school, I desperately wanted to fit in with a group of girls, a close-knit clique. I tried to dress like them, wearing similar outfits, emulating their style and their habits. Although I had my own style and identity, I wanted to change who I was and be like them. I tried to talk like them and even act like them. Why? Because I wanted to be accepted. My efforts were pointless and meaningless. They were a nice group of girls and were never mean to me. But I just couldn't do enough to truly feel like I belonged. The reality is, you can't please everyone, neither should you try.

I never got past a couple of Friday night movie invitations and post-football game welcome calls for burgers at a local restaurant. Each of the girls fit together in a perfect puzzle, and my piece wasn't cut from the same picture. I could try to force my piece into the puzzle, but perhaps, that's how not God intended it. Perhaps, I wasn't supposed to fit in with that particular puzzle.

During my senior year, things changed. I was no longer on the dance team with the girls because my afternoons became filled with working my first corporate job. Unbeknownst to me, God strategically altered the situation and separated me from what I thought I needed. He is so wise! I was entering a new and exciting season and was no longer around them at all. I thought I needed their validation and acceptance. I soon realized I didn't. I loved my new job, and was so fulfilled! Not every seventeen-year-old was earning their own income and growing as a businesswoman, but I was. This piece of the puzzle wasn't so bad after all. I was where I was destined to be. My desire, or what I now call my "disease to please," got me nowhere. And it shouldn't have; I wasn't supposed to fit in there.

We all desire acceptance; it's fundamental to our existence as humans. Reality TV shows are built on underlying issues and conflicts around acceptance. She wants to fit in with this group and does anything to be accepted. He wants her to choose him to be the one at whatever cost. It's common in our society. Children continually desire approval from their parents and peers. Employees are energized by recognition and accolades from their supervisors and superiors. Even Grandmother wants to know that she isn't forgotten and is loved. Belonging and being socially accepted is a basic human need.

I've seen this need to belong in churches many times. And to be honest, I've been guilty of it myself. Just recently, in our Women's class, I asked for the women to share prayer requests and needs that were concerning the group. I opened my prayer, being calm and collected, thanking God for the day and for allowing us to come to service. I thanked Him for Jesus and the opportunity to pray to Him. But somewhere shortly after the thanksgiving, my voice elevated, and I began to pace the floor next to the podium in the front of the room. I cried out to God on behalf of the women and their petitions. I was passionate in my prayer, and tears began to roll down my face. I could hear the responses and "Amens" of the women agreeing with me in prayer. But when I finished my conversation with God, a thought came to my mind. *You prayed too hard for this setting. You don't pray like the other women.* The disease to please began to infiltrate my thoughts, and my focus shifted from praying in the presence of God to pleasing His people in church on a Sunday afternoon.

People's Rejection

Attempting to please people is a recipe for disaster. Not a natural disaster but a personal one. Here's why: we aren't called to please people. We aren't called to live *for* people's approval. Therefore, whenever we project a desire for acceptance onto a person rather than God, rejection is most likely the outcome. Oftentimes, the person from whom we're seeking validation doesn't have the capacity to be what we're looking for; thus, we end up with a void. We end up feeling empty and lonely like no one cares about us. As real and valid as those feelings and emotions are, it is impossible for others to give us what we want.

Imagine you need a million dollars. This money would help you to pursue your passions and realize your dreams. It's a high price, but it's actually what you believe you need. So you go to a friend and ask her to loan you a million dollars. Unless your friend is an heir to a fortune or has recently won the lottery, she simply doesn't have the million dollars to give you.

How do you respond? Storm off? Feel rejected? You might feel a void, because your need for the money wasn't met. But did your friend cause the void? Absolutely not! Your expectation of her to fulfill a need in your life is outside of her ability.

This might be an extravagant example, but it perfectly illustrates how we navigate life: expecting others to accept us, validate us, affirm us. Our validation and acceptance is not their role or responsibility. Their inability to fulfill our expectations of them will most likely leave us feeling rejected.

We are the inheritance of God, and He always accepts us, without question and bias. It doesn't matter where we're from or what family we were born into; His acceptance remains the same. Likewise, it doesn't matter what we've done or where we've been, He still accepts us. His approach and disposition are not like other people's. People tend to accept us until we do something they disagree with, or something more important to them comes along. Then we are left wondering where, or if, we fit into their lives. Often, we are left feeling rejected and disappointed. God's acceptance is consistent and unconditional, never leaving us rejected or disappointed.

In my senior year of college and on the brink of graduation, I was confident of myself—what I had accomplished and where I was going in life. Yet, I still longed to be accepted. A few other girls and I had just finished a fund-raising event for a project in which we had raised over a thousand dollars—a big achievement for college students at that time. After our long evening, we were settling in at one of the girls' apartments when we received word of an altercation involving one of our friends. Wanting to be accepted, I rode along with the boisterous group to the location of the ruckus. All the while I thought, "Why am I doing this? Jumping into the middle of this dispute is not who I am." By the time we arrived at the location, I'd come to myself and decided I wasn't going to participate in the altercation. I had much more on the line than pleasing a few girls. However, my delayed decision came with a cost. Once everything ended, the girls resented my disengagement and rejected me. They didn't reject me for a few days or weeks. It has been years, and a true reconciliation still hasn't taken place.

Trying to fit in with the girls shouldn't have been my goal. However, because I was trying to please others and give too much of my power to people who had no right to it, I was rejected. However, I brought these feelings on myself simply because I wanted to be included in something that I honestly was already a part of. This was not their fault at all. It was mine. Their opinions of me shouldn't have mattered to me. If they didn't accept me for simply being me, did I really want to be in their company? I definitely shouldn't have.

Something had to change. I couldn't continue trying to live to please other people. I had to stop selling myself short. This saying puts it well: "We buy things we don't need with money we don't have to impress people we don't like." There is so much truth to that statement. I knew there had to be a better way—a way that would free me of concerning myself with the opinions of others. I needed to solely live for God. He was the only One that mattered and could affirm me better than anyone else. This meant resisting the disease to please and seeking ways that honored Him. In a world with several billion people, I only needed to live to gain the approval of One: God.

When I decided to Live for One, in the natural, life was the same. No huge change transpired in my life. Friendships and relationships were the same. Connections and ties didn't necessarily change, but I changed my perspective. I changed my mindset. I stopped striving to please people and desired to please God. If anyone else benefited from this revelation, that was great. Nevertheless, I needed this change for me. I needed to know that I didn't have to go out of my way to please anyone else. Simply because I am enough for God.

You Are Here for God

We are to live for One. "Finally, dear brothers and sisters, we urge you in the name of the Lord Jesus to live in a way that pleases God" (1 Thess. 4:1 NLT). We should strive to please only One person: God. His opinion and acceptance are all that matter. When I learned this truth, I experienced fresh freedom. I was invigorated. I did not need to please anyone else. I had to please only God. People's expectations of me or, should I say, what I thought they expected from me, constantly changed. Was I supposed to be thick, or was it okay that God made me thin? Was I supposed to be a successful independent woman, or was I supposed to be a submissive, quiet-as-a-mouse young lady? Was I supposed to hang out on the weekends with my peers, or was it okay that my weekends were spent at home reading, watching a movie or spending time with God? Seriously, what was I supposed to do? Can you see why I was relieved and felt free when I realized that I needed to please only God? My mom always told me not to worry about what other people think. She tried to ingrain this into me at a young age, but it wasn't until I was ready to believe it that I grasped and held close what she had imparted like precious pearls.

Learning this lesson, I had to rely on the power of the Holy Spirit, the third person in the Trinity (Father, Son, Holy Spirit) who dwells within believers. Many people refer to the Holy Spirit as one's conscience. For me, pleasing God and living for Him, meant actively listening to the Holy Spirit. "But the Helper, the Holy Spirit, whom the Father will send in my name, he will teach you all things and bring to your remembrance all that I have said to you" (John 14:26).

I was no longer concerned with what everyone else was doing or how they were living. I just wanted to listen to the voice of the Holy Spirit and allow Him to tell me how I should live my life. The wonderful thing about that was that I did not have to answer to anyone else. I no longer sought another's opinion. No other validation was necessary. It was simply me trusting His voice speaking to my heart. And I did. And I do. I trust the Holy Spirit.

Cultivate Your Relationship with God

I've been in several relationships, and I'll talk more about them in Lesson 3. In each relationship, I desired to make the best of it. I wanted my significant other to know that I was "in to" him, that I cared about him. Therefore, I was intentional about cultivating my relationship with him: getting to know him, listening to what he was saying even when he didn't say it directly, learning who he really was, and doing what he liked to do. I did these things because I cared about him and wanted to grow with him. Also, I wanted him to be pleased with me and my efforts to be with him. Just as I desired to grow in my relationship with my significant other, the most important connection to cultivate is my relationship with God. So often we are consumed with pleasing people who don't really matter in the long-term. But God's affirmation is what matters. It is eternal.

Daily devotions are vital to cultivating your relationship with God. It's intentional time set aside to read the Word, pray, worship, or journal. What you do during this time isn't as important as solely focusing on God and removing any distractions.

Some mornings you may focus on worshipping, while other mornings you read and memorize scriptures. Whichever you decide, the goal is to bask in His presence. Spend time with God. Often, our lives are so busy that we forfeit this important part of our day. However, when you spend quality time with God, it will manifest in your life. Because you can't please Him if you aren't spending time with Him and learning what He desires.

Her Audience of One

The gospel of Luke unveils the story of the woman with an alabaster box. Luke doesn't reveal her name, so we are compelled to focus on what she did rather than who she is. On a particular day, Jesus was in the house of Simon the Pharisee having dinner with many of his friends and disciples. Her appearance in this setting was quite strange. A woman would not enter someone's home uninvited, especially a woman with her reputation—a prostitute. I'm sure many of the men there knew her from her past. Perhaps they'd had personal encounters with her. But on that day, none of that mattered to her. As she approached Jesus, center stage, her performance was for an audience of One. It didn't matter who else was there or what they thought about her.

With a small flask in her hand and head tipped downward to ignore the stares and murmurs of the guests, she approached

Jesus. After all, His was the only approval she sought. She knew what others thought of her, and if she caught one of the men's gazes, she might have rethought her decision. Their private and personal thoughts of her were just that, their thoughts. They were nothing for her to be concerned with. And as she drew closer to Jesus, I imagine her thinking, "Surely, Jesus will accept my act of worship. I've made it this far; hopefully, He knows I want only His approval."

She was on a mission. She poured the oil from her flask onto Jesus's feet. Overwhelmed with emotion, tears fell down her face. She gathered her long black hair to dry Jesus's feet. This was her act of worship. It was between her and Jesus. The performance was for only Him. She had pleased people all of her life, and it had gotten her nowhere. Now, she wanted to please only Jesus. Other men may have mattered in the past, but at that moment, and every moment to come, this man Jesus was the only person who mattered to her.

After this woman's adoration, some of the men began to question her acts and Jesus's acceptance of her. She then heard Jesus say to her, "Your faith has saved you. Go in peace." His words were the best she had ever received. His were the words she had come all this way for.

Lesson Three
Live through Disappointments

Sometimes what we think is a disappointment, is really God getting us in position to go to a new level.

Joel Osteen

I have told you these things, so that in me you may have peace. In this world, you will have trouble. But take heart! I have overcome the world.

John 16:33

A lesson I had to learn is that disappointment and frustration are inevitable.

Everyone will face disappointment at some time in life, and to think that you are immune from disappointment only sets yourself up for further disappointment. When going through difficult situations, you should try to understand the lesson God is trying to teach you. There are times when you shouldn't ask God, "Why me?" but instead ask "Why not me?" We shouldn't expect circumstances in our lives to always occur as we want them. Why don't we expect God's will to sometimes (most times) differ from our will? Why don't we expect disappointment? Human nature is to want what we want, when we want it, and how we want it.

Being the firstborn child, I have some spoiled tendencies. Never mind that, I am spoiled. (There. I said it.) At a young age, I didn't do very well with disappointment. It's one of my flaws I've had to confront and work on over the years. I always wanted my life to go a certain way, and that "certain way" was my way. So when events or circumstances deviated from my plan, I was disappointed. My tendency to feel disappointed is partly because I'm used to getting what I want, but even more so because I'm passionate. Many of my disappointments have resulted from relationships I was passionate about. Whether with friends or with family or significant others, I've experienced many disappointments because something I was hoping to last a lifetime, or at least a long time, came to an end.

Unmet expectations led to deep disappointments in my life, and when the reality of unmet expectations sets in, we have to make a choice. One choice is to dwell on the hurt and thus live defeated. Sometimes not only does this feel like the easier choice, but it is the easier choice. It takes no effort or strength; it is a stagnant state that is simply comfortable. On occasion, I have chosen this state. Unfortunately, I'd much rather stay stuck because the push to get past the current circumstances seemed too difficult to fathom. My rationale sounds like this: Maybe if I stay here just a little longer, God will grant me that request. Perhaps, if I keep hoping and praying it will come to pass. I don't want to accept the reality that what I've hoped for, what I have planned in my mind isn't going to happen.

Often, I have had a pity party of one. I didn't need anyone to know the party was going on; it's a private party. But I partied, with music, tears, tissue, and thoughts of what could have been and what should have been replaying on the screen of my mind over and over and over again. It is a sad place to be in.

One Sunday morning I was in a low place. I'd just gotten off a cruise where I'd celebrated my birthday with friends. The Bahamas was lots of fun. I should have still been on a high, but I wasn't. I was low. I was sad. I was stuck. My hopes and expectations had been crushed and shattered. The relationship wasn't supposed to end. There were promises that had been made and hopes that were unfulfilled. We were supposed to be a couple. I was his rib. So why did the script just change from what we *both* wanted? Pain and hurt completely gripped me. And there I was in church that Sunday morning wailing. As I remember, it was pretty bad that day. This was my "public" pity party, and I could cry if I wanted to. What was only a few seconds felt like hours as I sat there wondering not only why it happened but why God allowed it to happen. I was fine before he entered my life. I didn't approach him; he reached out to me. Then he came with promises that I clung to for dear life. So why was the relationship changing? What was he moving on to without me?

In the midst of my thoughts, above the music and the congregants enjoying their praise break, I heard my dad speaking encouraging words in my ear. He knew why I was in that state, but he also knew that I couldn't stay physically or mentally in the state of disappointment.

While this despondent state I crawled into might be the easier choice, the alternative is a lot healthier and smarter.

The choice to get up and get over the disappointment is always the best choice. No doubt it can be more difficult, but it's the choice that implies that even though certain events in your life are not what you expected and you saw your life playing out differently, you trust God enough to work the situation out for your good and for His glory (Rom. 8:28).

Your Life Is Not Your Own

An unmet expectation may be a disappointment to me, but it's never a disappointment to God. It's funny because we live our lives with all of the dreams and plans we've conjured, but too often we never consult the Author or Playwright of our life story. That's like going to a movie or reading a book, and rather than seeing how the author intended the story to evolve, we decide to create our own ending. As creative as you may be, only the author can choose how the story ends. If it's a good story, your version probably isn't how the original unfolds. The reason is simple: you did not write it. Likewise, your life is not your own.

Our lives belong to God. Each of us has been given a unique life plan that isn't like anyone else's on this earth. No two plans are alike. No two lives are identical. Just as our fingerprints are unique, so are the strategic and intentional plans for our lives. We have to overcome the comparison trap that so desperately wishes to entangle us. Seeing someone else's plan and how God orchestrated her life, though we don't envy her, we think, "If that's how it turned out for her, then maybe my story will be similar." We view how long it took her to get married and think, "That's how it'll be for me." We watch how God uses his ministry and gift, and we think, "That's how my platform will unfold." We see how they grow their business or organization, and so we think if we do the same things ours will look exactly the same. That can't be any further from the truth. Our lives are tailor-made for us by God. He didn't create a standardized plan that will work for each of us. Each of us has a different plan, a different calling, a different life. We cannot plan them, we cannot write them, because thinking we own our lives will lead to disappointment. Our lives are not our own. We belong to God.

I've done it though. I've tried to work things out in my life that were outside of God's will, and I knew it wasn't what He desired. I knew what I was doing wasn't in His plan for me, at least not in that season. But I wanted my way. I wanted this re-lationship to work. I wanted it to last. So, for about six months, I gave it my all. I worked at it. I did all I knew to do, and then some, to make this relationship work. It didn't matter to me that it was a complete emotional roller coaster. I was willing to ride it out because he'd made promises. I was his better half. I was his rib, his missing piece. And so, because I believed what he'd promised, not what God said, I determined to make the relationship work. I so desperately needed it to work, because my life was on the line.

But God did not write this relationship in my story. He did not want this relationship for me. It wasn't in His plan. And because I was going against His plan, I was left disappointed, hurt, and distraught. Going outside of God's plan will do that, simply because our lives are not our own.

Be Content

"I have learned to be content regardless of my circumstances" (Phil. 4:11 BSB). It was freeing when I learned to be content with where I was and with what I had. Rather than looking at what others had and how others had progressed, I began to look at all that I had been blessed with and how far I'd progressed. And honestly, I was content with myself. I didn't have to long for someone else's life because I actually had a pretty good life, one I'm sure someone else would love to have. Being content meant accepting how God was writing my story. It's not perfect, but it's mine.

A quote I like to say is "There are things that only God can control, and I'm okay with that. Then there are things that He allows me to control, and He's okay with that." Knowing the difference between God's job and our job is vital to living a content life. If it's outside of our control, then there's no reason to concern ourselves with it. Concerning ourselves with what we don't have control over leads to disappointment. If it's outside of our sphere of influence, we have to stop worrying about it. Those concerns, problems, desires, and dreams belong to God, and however they unfold is completely up to Him. It's best to let it go. Let God be God, and you be who He designed you to be.

Barren but Blessed

One of my favorite stories in the Bible is that of the Shunammite woman found in 2 Kings 4. She was a strong woman of God. Her physical and spiritual strength were exemplified through her countless acts of service and honor toward others. She was a true servant, someone we should emulate. She demonstrated her strong faith when she realized the prophet Elisha had nowhere to stay while he was in town for ministry. No one had to tell her what needed to be done. She took the initiative and got it done. After consulting her husband, she prepared living quarters for Elisha on her rooftop so that he would have a comfortable place to dwell. Because she was a woman of great hospitality, I imagine that as she prepared meals for her husband, she also ensured the man of God was fed.

Elisha acknowledged this woman's hospitality and her respect for his ministry. He asked his servant to call in the Shunammite woman. He desired to bestow a blessing on this woman and asked her what he could do for her. The Shunammite woman said, "I dwell among my people." In other words, she wanted him to know that she was content. She'd accepted the story that God had written for her life and was in a good place.

However, Elisha knew there had to be more to her story. He asked his servant to suggest what the prophet could do for this gracious, hospitable woman. Now Elisha learns that the Shunammite woman is barren, a childless wife.

Most women in this condition would likely have asked for their heart's desire. I would have. The disappointment of barrenness would have been the first thing mentioned. But she didn't allow her disappointments of childlessness to cause her to be discontent. She was content with herself. She was content with her husband, and she was content with serving the man of God. Certainly, she desired a child, but she'd found peace and contentment with how God was writing her life. As a result, God blessed her by opening her womb and giving her a child.

Even in our longings and disappointments, we can find contentment. This state of being does not negate the current circumstances of our lives but rather trusts that God's plan and will are sovereign. Many times, what we desire from God is on the other side of contentment. It's on the other side of relinquishing our disappointment to Him and trusting that He knows what's best for us. "No good thing will he withhold from them that walk uprightly" (Psalm 84:11 KJV).

Healing Is a Process

A song came out in the '90s that expressed, "Emotions make you cry sometimes, emotions make you sad sometimes, emotions make you glad sometimes, but most of all they make you fall in love." Emotions. You cannot always look at someone's physical appearance and see that they're hurting emotionally. Often, they wear a smile and respond the Christian way, "I'm blessed and highly favored." But in actuality they are not okay; they are hurting emotionally. Maybe a loved one has left them—through walking away or in death. Or perhaps their spouse's love has grown cold. Maybe loneliness is causing this emotional hurt. Not feeling included or wanted or loved. So they're left with emotional hurt. I truly believe that emotional hurt hits every person in the body of Christ at least once in their lives. The hurt might not look the same, but I'm sure we've all experienced a need for healing from disappointment.

After going through such deep disappointment in my life, I needed to be healed. My heart was crushed, my feelings were hurt, and for a long time, I didn't realize the damage I'd done to myself. Days, weeks, months, and years passed, and I felt stuck. Normally, I could bounce back from most kinds of emotional hurts, but this relationship break was different. I couldn't get over it. I wanted to, but something kept me bound to the hurt, bound to the pain. Part of me wanted to get over it, and part of me wanted the relationship back to the way it was, or the way I thought it was.

I had the privilege of traveling the world for my job as an accountant for an oil and gas company here in Houston. It was during my trip to Equatorial Guinea while lying beside the pool one evening after work, that God spoke to me through His Word about my situation in which I was hurting—not physically hurting but emotionally. I wasn't depressed, I wasn't necessarily sad, but my heart needed healing. As I lay next to the hotel pool, I was reminded of the story of the lame man at the pool of Bethesda (John 5:5–8).

I heard Jesus speak to my Spirit: *Constance, do you want to be made whole?* It didn't matter what had happened, or who was at fault. It didn't matter how many times people brought it up, or how I thought the relationship should have turned out. God was asking me if I wanted healing from the hurt. A lot of times we cannot heal emotionally because our excuses get in the way. But God is Jehovah Rapha, the God who heals. Not only does He heal cancer and disease, not only does He heal ailments and sickness, but He has the power to heal every single emotion that is keeping us from living a full and abundant life. But we must get rid of excuses that are hindering our healing.

We also have to want to be healed! My spiritual mother says that all the time, "Pray for your 'want to'." Too often we don't want to let go of our sorrow. We derive a strange satisfaction from wallowing in our hurts. Change is a decision we have to make. We have to want to be whole. Some people constantly nurse their wounds and are addicted to their afflictions. They aren't ready to be made whole. They're having pity parties and want a long guest list. They've gotten comfortable in this emotionally sick place. How is it that two people can go through the exact same tragedy but look totally different? One person is continuing to live out purpose and calling, while the other is sad, depressed, and feels rejected. The difference is not Jesus and His power to heal; the difference is the individual. We have to want to. 'Wanting to' is a conscious decision that says, "Regardless of what I've been through, I'm going to keep pressing on." 'Wanting to' says, "It doesn't feel good when I wake up every morning, but I'm sure glad I woke up." 'Wanting to' says, "I hate that this has happened to me, but the reason I am still here is because there is purpose and destiny for me." To heal emotionally, we have to want to. Jesus is asking you, "Do you *want* to be made whole?"

The resource I attribute my ultimate healing, besides God and the Holy Spirit, is 21 Day Inner Healing Journey by Jimmy Evans and Marriage Today (www.marriagetoday.com).

Lesson Four
Live and Learn

Learn from yesterday, live for today and hope for tomorrow.

Albert Einstein

I press on toward the goal to win the prize for which God has called me heavenward in Christ Jesus.

Philippians 3:14

A lesson I had to learn is that I'm either entering a storm, in the midst of a storm or exiting a storm.

In 2008, life was great. That August I had graduated from Sam Houston State University with a Master of Business Administration and began working at a Big Four accounting firm in September. Life was indeed great. However, I was entering a season that would challenge my faith. My next career step was to earn my professional certification for my field, accounting. As a Certified Public Accountant (CPA), I needed to pass all four parts of the exam within eighteen months. I could do this! Always on the Honor Roll, a member of the National Honor Society, and on the Dean's List all throughout college, I would pass this exam with ease!

As I prepared to take the first CPA exam in November, my confidence and determination floated at an ultimate high. I sat for the test and anticipated passing results. However, I didn't pass the exam. Not only did I fail the first exam, I failed several more after that. I couldn't figure out what was happening or much less why. Failing the exams was not part of my plan. While my confidence and determination wavered, I knew God was going to help me get through this difficult storm.

So I tested and trusted, but for two long, tiring years, I never saw a passing score. Then it seemed as though the heavens opened in 2010 when I passed my first exam. I was excited, grateful, and filled with hope all at the same time. I remember the day I received the results, a 95. All I could do was cry and thank God.

Yet my journey was not over. Although I passed my second exam in August 2011, I failed my subsequent exams. Seriously! Talk about wanting to give up and throw in the towel. I was there! I was growing weary. I took a break from taking the exam and thought about other options. But I was reminded of Philippians 1:6 "He that began a good work in you will bring it to completion." So I stayed in the race, even after I lost the credit for the first exam, which meant I'd have to retest it.

If I was going to successfully pass the CPA exams, I was going to have to lean on God and surrender to Him. I could not do it on my own. In August 2012, four years after I began this journey, rather than just study the testing material, I concentrated on growing my relationship with God and studying His Word. Finally, in October 2012, I passed my final exam. To God be the glory. As I reflect on the four-year journey, I can't help but thank God for allowing me to go through this difficult period in order to show me who He is. I received my CPA license on June 15, 2013, in Austin, Texas. It was not just me who accomplished this but my heavenly Father, who spoke to my storm and said, "Peace be still."

The Storm Won't Last

The four-year period spent preparing for the exam seemed like forever. As the days, months, and years passed, I thought I'd never reach success. It was like I was in the midst of a storm with no help in sight. The wind and the waves made it difficult to navigate. It seemed so much easier to wave the white flag of surrender than to keep pressing on in this hard, difficult, seemingly impossible journey. When you're in a difficult situation, doesn't it feel like the struggle will never end, that all hope is lost and you'll never see a brighter day? However, as much as it seems to the contrary, the storm will not last forever. Regardless of the types of storms I've experienced, none have lasted forever. They all came to an end: the relationship storm, the CPA storm, the workplace storm, the family storm. All storms have a termination date. Trust me; your storm has a termination date, too.

Life's storms are inevitable. We all will go through storms, and none of us are exempt or immune to the crashing waves and thunderous wind and pounding rain. Although everyone will go through a storm, not everyone knows how to endure a storm. Some people allow the waves to overtake them, not only because their personal winds are strong and powerful, but because they are not equipped to endure the storm brewing in their lives. Some take flight at the first hint of a coming storm, refusing to believe that the storm won't last forever. But peace will come. So dust off your raincoat and boots, because, though the storm might get bad, it will not overtake you.

It's also important to have the right perspective to endure our storms. We have two options: a positive attitude about the storm or a negative one. It's really that simple. There's no in-between. It's either or. During the four-year period in which I labored to prepare for the exam, I had to stay positive if I wanted to pass. Negative energy and negative vibes were not going to make the storm end any sooner. The best approach was not only to endure it but to endure it well, with a positive attitude. Not liking the storm does not mean we're being negative. We don't have to like what we're experiencing, but we should remain positive. Regardless of how difficult our situation seems, how impossible it appears that circumstances will change, what has already transpired, or what statistics say, having a positive perspective allows us to focus on the good around us, even in the midst of trying times.

Philippians 4:4 compels us to "Rejoice always," and therein is where we find positivity. Preparing for the CPA exam was very difficult. But even in the midst of setbacks and deep dis-appointments, I had to find something worth celebrating. For example, if I didn't pass the test, I celebrated that my score was a little higher than the previous one. If my score wasn't higher, I celebrated that I had enough courage to take the test again. If I decided not to take the test, I celebrated that I was still study-ing. And even if I took a break from studying, I celebrated that I hadn't completely given up. When I began this journey, I didn't know it would take me four years. If I'd waited to cel-ebrate only when I'd gotten passing results, I would have lost hope long before I took that last test. But because I rejoiced about even small accomplishments or decisions along the way, the storm was much more bearable.

Find mini celebratory moments on the way to your goal. How-ever small it might be, it's important to celebrate it. Make a big deal when you hold your tongue rather than retaliate. Cel-ebrate when you pass up that warm, chocolate dessert even when your weight-loss battle has gone on too long. Make a big deal when you end the day without tears or a meltdown. You can always find a positive perspective; you just have to look for it, even if it's a mini success. The storm won't be as bad if you're intentional about celebrating along the way.

Trust the Process

God has a unique process for each of us. I recall a picture that shows a straight line starting at point A and ending at B. Next to it is a squiggly, mixed-up line going from A to B. The caption read something like "Your Plan vs. God's Plan." It's true. Often, when we set a goal or desire something, we expect the process to be smooth. Sorry, but life is rarely smooth. To reach our final destination, we are sure to encounter detours, pit stops, and bumps along the way. Nevertheless, we have to trust the process. As long as God is leading us, we can have confidence that His way is better than our ways, and His thoughts better than our thoughts (Isa. 55:8–9).

Suffering and setbacks are part of a greater process that lead to success. God doesn't allow us to suffer for nothing. He promises that "All things work together for good to those who love God, to those who are called according to His purpose" (Rom. 8:28 NKJV). "All things" include bad incidents, dry seasons, down moments, frustrations. And it means the good stuff, too. God will take all of it and make it worth the headache and heartache. Everything we experience in life, even the unfavorable events we wish we didn't have to go through, are all a part of the process. And we must trust the process.

We can kick and scream as we're in the midst of the process, but that won't make the experience easier or change the situation. It will usually prolong the journey and make it much more difficult to endure. The reason is that God wants to teach us something in the process. Maybe we need patience, so we're going through the process to learn how to wait patiently. Perhaps the process is intended to teach you grace. So you learn to give grace to others because of the process you're enduring. Maybe the process is to teach you persistence because for too long giving up and quitting have been your norm. You learn grit and to keep going until the end because of the process God has for you. Trust that God is taking you through your specific process for a reason, even if you don't understand it right away.

My CPA process taught me many things, one of which was never, ever give up. I knew that eventually if I kept trying, kept praying, kept studying I would pass. Now as I enter different seasons in life, I don't give up until I reach my goal. Quitting is not an option for me because I've gone through a process that taught me to persist. Even when completing tasks or reaching goals take longer than expected, I don't quit. I pray and believe until I reach my goal, or God redirects me to something better. I'm reminded of what one of my pastors said: "Nothing is oftentimes the first sign of a miracle." If I have to keep going to God, I will, because after nothing there's bound to be a miracle. That's what happened when Ahab kept checking to see if rain was coming in 1 Kings 18. Eventually, after the drought, an outpouring of rain and blessings came. If something's going to give, it won't be me.

My CPA exam experience also taught me humility. It was very humbling to continually receive failing results. Passing tests used to come easy for me in grade school and college, but I had to learn humility and let go of every ounce of pride I had. When you've always been the crème de la crème, you get a little embarrassed when you fail. God needed to show me humility.

But, most important, the process taught me trust. I could not pass on my own. I needed to trust God's plan and know that He would help me pass. I had to trust that He knew what He was doing. As much as I wanted to help God, I couldn't because I trusted Him. The test taught me that God is in complete control and that "he would not withhold any good thing from me" (Ps. 84:11). I hadn't passed when I expected to pass because it was not what God wanted for me at that time. And I had to completely trust Him. If you don't have what you want or are expecting from God right now, then perhaps it's not for you to have in this season. It's a hard reality to face, a hard pill to swallow. But get a bigger glass of water and drink up.

Jekalyn Carr sings the song "You Will Win." It talks about the obstacles that come against us, but in the end, we will win. If you knew you were destined to win, would you endure the process with more confidence? Would you take the journey with more zeal and passion because it was already foretold that you would be victorious? Well, the truth is, you will win. The process may not be what you expected, and the journey might not be what you desired. Nevertheless, there is a promise in the process and joy for the journey because you will win. The question is, do you believe it? Do you believe that, though the process you're going through may be difficult, you have the potential to win? You just have to believe you will.

Persistence Pays Off

In the gospel of Luke, Jesus tells a parable about a persistent widow. As I read the story, she reminded me of myself. She refused to take no for an answer because she knew she had the potential to win her case. This woman had gone to a powerful judge, expecting justice for her situation because she knew her legal rights. The judge, with all of his power and authority, had compassion neither on her nor the concerns she continually brought before him. Thus, each time she went to him pleading for justice, he turned her away. She nagged him, annoyed him, got on his last nerve; however, none of her attempts to get relief and justice were successful. But this woman resolved that she wouldn't give up. Whereas some people would retreat at the wicked, arrogant, unjust judge's orders, she was persistent. It was her tenacity and determination that caused the judge to finally grant her request. Essentially, he wanted her to leave him alone, and the only way that would happen is if he gave her what she wanted.

Jesus is teaching through this parable that "we should always pray and not give up or faint" (Luke 18:1). If this powerless person could eventually receive justice from a powerful judge, we, being heirs of God, can request in prayer what we desire from Him and, if it is His will, expect our requests to be granted. The Bible doesn't tell us how many times the woman went to the judge, it just says "for some time." Maybe it was five times, or an entire week, month, or year. We really don't know, and she didn't know how long it would take, either. I can imagine that during her first appearance before the judge, she was dressed up and possessed supporting documents to vindicate her request. She couldn't have had any idea that this process would take as long as it did. Likely, she expected a quick response. Regardless of how long it took to get what she desired, she was committed to the goal. Obstacles, opposition, and oppression were not enough to stop this woman of extreme faith and determination.

Persistence pays off. When you enter every situation with the mind-set that you will win, you will. Defeat cannot be an option. Too many people give up too soon because God has delayed in their situation. When you are expecting God to do something that aligns with His will, the only viable option is success. It must be victory. This whole parable is about persistent prayer, and James 5:16 says, "The effectual fervent prayer of the righteous [avails] much" (KJV). If you know God has the power to change your situation, why would you not go to Him for what you need or desire? He's not like the judge in the parable, though; He wants to see you win, but He also wants to see how much faith you possess during the delays and detours of life. The persistent widow was not going to leave until she received what she deserved, not because she was spoiled and wanted her way, but because she knew what was due her and what she could have.

Even in the storms and difficult seasons of life, you will always win. The process may be difficult, but it will be well worth the journey when you see victory on the other side.

Lesson Five
Live Out Loud

Preach the Gospel at all times, and if necessary use words.

St. Francis of Assisi

In the same way, let your light shine before others, that they may see your good deeds and glorify your Father in heaven.

Matthew 5:16

A lesson I had to learn is that opportunities will always present themselves for me to show who I really am.

We will always have chances to remove our masks, take off the makeup, and allow our true characters, the essence of who we are, to be revealed. When you were very young, probably before you can remember, you learned a song. Perhaps you learned it at home, or maybe at a babysitter's, or even in a daycare. We all learned the Alphabet song. Not only did *you* learn it, but your parents also learned it. If we were to take a trip to any daycare in your city and peek into one of the classrooms, we'd most likely find teachers singing the ABCs along with their students. This song is timeless. It will never change because the characters don't change. The alphabet will always have the same twenty-six characters. We use them in a variety of arrangements to create words and sentences, type an essay or craft a song, or write a book.

The alphabet didn't change from elementary to middle school to high school, but each year you built on what you learned the previous year. That's how it is with your life and character. Your character, the essence of who you are, is ingrained in your being. Character is the commitment to a set of values and beliefs you will not compromise or waver on in any given situation. Situations and circumstances, events you've seen and experienced, your home environment and the friends with whom you associate, your relationship with God and the music you enjoy are all factors that build your character. You don't wake up one morning and are instantly the ideal person with perfect character. Your character is built over time. So when forced with a decision, you have the power to choose how you will allow it to shape your character.

Many circumstances will challenge your character. Oftentimes, your wants and desires will unexpectedly conflict with your character. Perhaps you want a particular job, but the job description, environment, or culture do not align with your character. Do you take the job or keep a position that you don't want but is what you think you need to earn a living? Maybe it's not a job but a relationship. You desire to be with a certain person, but when you're together, you're not your true self. The person you are—or say you are—will often be challenged regarding your dreams and desires.

I've done some things that were completely outside of my character because the desire to have what I longed for was stronger than the values and principles I'd set for myself. It's not that I'm a bad person or that I don't have morals and values. I did what I normally would not do because, at that moment, I placed a higher value on what I wanted than I did on my character. It's hard to admit, but it is true. However, the upside is that those instances were simply moments. They didn't change my character or who I was. Right?

Well, I thought what I'd done was just an action with no consequences. But, truly, those small actions, if done repeatedly, become habits, which then have the power to shape me—for good or bad. Habits are actions, thoughts, and attitudes we do on a regular basis without thinking about it. They become our custom and pattern. Studies have shown that it can take as little as twenty-one days to form a habit. Habits eventually become part of our character, who we are on the inside. Then our character becomes our destiny. But it all starts with the small actions we do every day.

Don't Get Out of Character

I had no idea that when a friend offered me a job as one of the top executives for a small corporation that this situation would challenge my character. In all honesty, as I considered taking the position, I was not at peace. Something didn't seem right about my transitioning into this role at this time. The job meant a better title and higher pay. But because I didn't have peace, I should have refused the offer, stayed where I was, and waited patiently for God to open a door. Sadly, I didn't wait. I nervously accepted the offer. What a costly decision! I learned that it's vital to always follow peace. Even if it doesn't make sense to refuse an opportunity that appears to be favorable, if you don't have peace about it walk away. Following peace is the best option. Like the song says: "Oh what peace we often forfeit." It sounds crazy that we'd give up peace, but we do it all the time. It's like we can't resist the lure of better benefits, higher pay, more accolades. The alternative to peace beckons us, while peace is not pushy and allows us to choose what could possibly destroy us. Why do we fall for that? Why did I do that?

Within two short weeks, after I accepted this new role, I realized my huge mistake. But it was too late. There was no turning back. I'd made a choice, and now my character was challenged. I couldn't say I didn't see it coming, because I had no peace from the first interaction. However, I resolved at that moment that my character would exude in every conversation, discussion, email, and phone call. I was not going to allow the difficult circumstances to take me out of character. This was hard because I was dealing with a friend, but I had to endure this season of my life.

Every day on the way to work I prayed that God would be with me and that my character would not be tarnished or compromised. Most days I entered the office with confidence and grace—confident that I would be successful in all of my endeavors, and grace to give as often as needed. Those character traits were needed in the midst of this oppressive work environment. Other days, however, though I felt anxious about the day's events, I quickly resolved to change my thought process because positive feelings would always sustain me. I had to "take every thought captive" (2 Cor. 10:5). One can only draw from what is within when difficult circumstances arise. If one possesses bitterness and resentment, then he or she will express bitterness and resentment.

My friend expected me to retaliate, but that wasn't in my character. Most times I offered no reaction, which I am sure was more upsetting to her than if I had struck back in some way. When positive characteristics, like joy and gratitude, are constant dispositions, then that's what we will demonstrate. I created a screen saver on my computer that said, "Count It All Joy." Every time I looked at my desktop, I was reminded to find the joy in all situations. Do not give people or circumstances power over your thoughts and mind, the power to take you out of who you are and change you. Nothing should have that much power over you. You choose your response and how you will feel. Needless to say, anything or anyone who threatens your character should be removed from your life. Keeping them around is toxic to who you are and who God has destined you to be. Remember "Bad company corrupts good character" (1 Cor. 15:33). Outside forces matter.

Our natural tendency is to protect ourselves. We don't want to become susceptible to emotional harm and allow it to go unaddressed. We want people to respect and appreciate us. Retaliation and vindication can seem to be the right answer. However, in doing so, it's important to respect ourselves and appreciate the person God created us to be.

Eventually, that season of my life ended. The dust settled. The smoke cleared. At the end of the road, I stood with my character intact. Shortly after, I spoke to a colleague who marveled at my calmness while daily facing adversity at my workplace. She saw the injustices, but she also saw how I responded. I professed to be a Christian and played gospel music on my computer every day, thus my words and actions needed to align with my belief. I did not want someone to stumble because of me. I feel like God gave me a big "Well done."

Godly character is a matter of the heart. Out of the heart flows the issues of life (Prov. 4:23). The heart is where your innermost thoughts, motives, ideas—your character—reside. To know a person's character is to understand their heart and intent. However, God is the only one who can truly examine our hearts, and He evaluates every intent and motive. "Living out loud" means living with a heart that is pleasing to God; one where God's Spirit is welcomed to dwell and His Word is inscribed. When God's Word is in your heart, a result of spending time studying and meditating, it shows in your character. I didn't get out of character at that company, not because I had willpower or patience, but because I allowed God's Word to live in my heart. There was a time when I did get out of character at a different job, but that's another story for another day.

Do the Right Thing

When presented with the opportunity to do right or wrong, most morally sound people like to think they choose to do right. However, the truth is we are all guilty of willingly and knowingly doing the wrong thing. When given a choice between right and wrong, we rethink the options and choose between right and *convenient*. The option may not be illegal, but it's more convenient than doing what is right. It's convenient to live together. It's convenient to take longer lunch breaks. It's convenient not to pay a tithe. It is convenient to sleep in rather than to clean the house. It's convenient to drive over the speed limit when you can't be late. (Yeah, that's me.) Rather than doing the right thing, people rationalize why what's convenient is their personal "right." *Wrong!* Society has for a very long time bought into the lie that it's okay to choose convenience over correctness, and now that value shows in our relationships, homes, churches, communities, and governments. It's sad, but convenience has become more acceptable than righteousness.

Choosing right over convenience or wrong reminds me of driving in Houston, Texas, which is ranked number four for the worst traffic in America. Our city has such heavy traffic because of a large number of vehicles on the road, which means lots of congestion, particularly the highways. Another option is to take a less populated route. Along with avoiding heavy traffic, you aren't distracted by billboards, bumper stickers, and vanity license plates, and you'll arrive at your destination in a less harried state of mind.

Just as you encounter fewer vehicles on the alternate route in Houston, fewer people may agree with you when you choose to do the right thing. Sometimes you may feel like you're the only one doing the right thing. That's because most people are on the more convenient, albeit congested, highway. On the alternate narrow road, you have more room to maneuver and get from your current location to your predestined calling. "Enter through the narrow gate. For wide is the gate and broad is the road that leads to destruction, and many enter through it" (Matt. 7:13 author's paraphrase). The road may be narrow, but on it, you'll find peace of mind. And peace is priceless! You'll have confidence that you'll get to your destination safely, without much fear or doubt. Oh, and you'll get there on time! In one of his lessons, Dr. J. Vernon McGee says, the "Broad-way" is always more enticing with its flashing lights and exotic shows. Nevertheless, it's the narrow way that God desires us to choose because He wants us to do the right thing.

Choose Wisdom

The Bible gives a glimpse of a confident, strong, and independent woman by the name of Abigail. She's a type A, I'll-get-the-job-done, woman. I definitely see myself in Abigail. If there's an issue, she resolves it and moves on. Her husband, Nabal, on the other hand, was anything but Type A. I guess it's a case of opposites attract. Though she was wise, he was a fool. I'm not demeaning the man; his name really means fool. As this story in 1 Samuel unfolds, David, the man of God, protected Nabal's sheep and shepherds. David didn't have to do this, but when he saw the danger, he took action. When David asked Nabal for a favor in return, Nabal dishonored the man of God. As a consequence of Nabal's foolishness, David set out with his followers to wipe out Nabal and his entire household. The choice Nabal made was about to cost him everything, even his life. (Can you imagine being married to a complete fool? That was Abigail's life.) Some choices we make have the potential to cost us our lives. It just takes one choice. Though David's anger overtook him, his actions were warranted because of Nabal's disrespect.

When news of these events reached Abigail, she went into action. She made a choice, and she chose wisdom. While she respected her husband (because that's always wise), she acknowledged that David was right in this situation. So she dealt with the issue that had angered David. She could have ignored the issue, but she resolved to do the right thing, for her life and family were at stake, too. Neither Nabal nor her household could keep her from doing what was right. Though David intended to wipe out the entire household, Abigail intercepted David's plan by providing him and his men with food and supplies, what they had initially requested. That's all they wanted. She chose to respectfully go against her husband, not bashing or degrading his authority, and do what was right not only in the sight of the king but also in the sight of God.

Every day you are faced with many choices. It could be on the job, where you're representing Christ in an oppressive environment, deciding to do what's right, even though you're facing an unjust situation. Perhaps you'll have opportunities in your church to address circumstances in which certain accommodations are being made away from Christ and His Word in favor of human convenience. You will inevitably encounter opportunities in your family to stand up against sins that have become generational patterns—actions, words, and thinking that are wrong yet are accepted. You may have opportunities in your friendships to avoid gossip, backstabbing, deception, and pride. In all opportunities you come across, doing the right thing will pay off. Even if it seems more convenient to do the alternative, choose wisely.

Nabal, Abigail's husband, died of a stroke shortly after this encounter with David. I can't help but think that his foolishness caused his premature death. Meanwhile, David recognized that Abigail was a wise, respectful woman. She honored the man of God. When David heard of Nabal's death, he quickly asked Abigail to marry him. I guess he didn't want anyone to choose her first. He admired and was attracted to her qualities of strength and wisdom. Choosing the right thing allowed her to be wed to a future king and man of God.

Let Your Actions Speak for You

Abigail met David with the food and supplies he had originally requested. She spoke to David about the iniquity of her husband and acknowledged his foolishness. She didn't stop there. She did not solely rely on her words. Abigail coupled her words with her actions. Her actions demonstrated her authenticity. She chose to get up and do what was necessary to sustain the man of God. She could have made a promise to David and told him she'd give it to him at a later date, but her actions revealed her heart and character. Abigail was a wise woman.

Words aren't always required. Our actions should speak just as loud. They should show what's in our hearts. Silently doing the right thing speaks more than trying to convince someone with words. I've had to learn this because I tend to want to explain and justify myself to people. I want them to know my heart and my side of the story. It could be the smallest thing, and I want to make sure I verbally conveyed my intentions. As I've matured, I've realized that vindicating myself isn't always necessary. People aren't convinced by our words; they're convinced by our actions. Too many people say one thing yet do another. Their actions don't align with what they profess. We know these people, and sometimes we are those people. It's time to let our actions speak for themselves. We must continually monitor our actions so that they align with our words. It's easy to make promises, it's easy to profess our faith, it's easy to say the right thing, but it takes a wise person to follow through with actions that coincide with their words. This is true especially when the alternative is more appealing or when we think justice will not be revealed. As with Abigail, when we do the right thing, we can always expect a greater blessing.

Lesson Six
*L*ive on *P*urpose

Use me, God. Show me how to take who I am,
who I want to be, and what I can do, and use it
for a purpose greater than myself.

Rev. Dr. Martin Luther King, Jr.

Many are the plans in a person's heart,
but it is the Lord's purpose that prevails.

Proverbs 19:21

A lesson I had to learn is to live on purpose.

Neither you nor I can effectively live as God intended unless we have a clear understanding of who He called us to be. People spend much time looking for purpose in external sources. They read books, research, take personality tests, and complete quizzes and assessments, but purpose can be revealed only by the One who manufactured you—God Himself. Before you were born, before you were the apple of your parents' eyes, before you took your first steps, God placed His purpose inside of you. To know your purpose, you must consult God.

Everything Leads to Purpose

A familiar children's story unfolds in this manner. Cinderella's mother and father had both passed away, and she's forced to live with her wicked stepfamily—her stepmother and two stepsisters. It has to be difficult for a child to lose a parent and then be forced to live with a stepfamily who couldn't care less about her. However, it is because of the pain she has experienced that she is positioned to live out her purpose. We all know how the story ends: she finds her Prince Charming. However, if she hadn't been an orphan whose parents died, if she hadn't been living with her stepmother and stepsisters, if she hadn't experienced all the hardships, she would not have been in the position to live out her purpose of becoming the princess. Everyone has experienced difficult circumstances that have tested us, but perhaps these circumstances positioned us for the purpose for which God has called us to.

Cinderella was made to work all day, cleaning, sewing, and cooking. She tried her best to make her stepmother and step-sisters happy. Despite her efforts to please, her stepsisters were cruel to her, and her stepmother was jealous of her. In the same manner, your purpose won't please everybody. There are times that people will even disagree with the purpose God has given you, and you have to accept this reality. If you've gone through a divorce and you believe your purpose is to speak into the lives of young married women, don't let anyone stop you. If you didn't go to college, but you are called to write a book, do it. Don't look for people to validate your God-given purpose, which He gave you to fulfill. Your purpose is God's plan, not man's. That's why Jeremiah 29:11 says, "I know the plans that I have for you." God knows what He's doing in your life, and if He gave you that purpose, don't be ashamed of it, don't let anyone talk down to you about it, don't even try to discourage yourself about it. Oftentimes, we are aware of our purpose but convince ourselves that we cannot operate in it.

Your purpose will not look like anyone else's because God uniquely designed it for you. My mother loves shopping. Me, not as much. When my sister and I were very young, my mother woke up on Saturday mornings, dressed us, and packed us in the car. We went to the mall and spent the whole day there. Not necessarily looking for anything in particular, we just browsed, window shopping from one end to the other. I feel like I have mall hours accumulated and don't need to spend much time in them today.

When I must go to the mall, as opposed to my preference for online shopping, I know what I'm looking for. I go into the store, get it, and leave. Not my mom. She spends lots of time trying on one piece of clothing after another. She has to see if this dress fits, if those shoes look right. She looks at it from this angle and that side. Your purpose is like trying on that outfit or piece of clothing in the dressing room. You have to try on this or that until you find the perfect fit. Sometimes what you're passionate about will lead you to your purpose. Other times, you will have to do what you're needed to do until you can do what you're purposed to do, as Beth Moore states. Don't give up on your purpose too soon. I guarantee you that if you keep trying different jobs, ministries, organizations, and such, you will realize your purpose and specific calling.

The Cinderella story continues with invitations sent to all the homes in the kingdom, inviting all of the girls to a ball. The prince is looking for a princess. At the ball, Cinderella catches the eye of the prince. She didn't go looking for him, yet he found her because she was walking in purpose. Your "purpose will promote you." When you are operating in your purpose, doors will open for you. Opportunities will become available. People who never knew you will speak your name. The Word of God says that your gift will make room for you (Prov. 18:16). If the gift is from God, it will make room for you and will promote you to platforms you would never have imagined. It still amazes me how many opportunities I've been given simply because I'm using my God-given gift effectively. It literally blows my mind, but my gift has made room for me and continues to do so.

I love that your gift will make room for you and you don't have to make room for your gift. I love that you don't have to tell everyone what you can do, for God strategically orchestrates opportunities for you at the right time. He sets it up that some-one will be looking for volunteers in your local church, and all of a sudden you are coordinating large events at the church. God works it that you share your story or your testimony in your small group, and as a result, you begin mentoring oth-er women and young ladies. Your gifts will make room for you, and God promotes and elevates you. Psalm 75:6 says that "promotion does not come from the east or the west or the south; it comes from God."

Why Are You Here?

Understanding why you are here and why you've been granted this day to live can sometimes be perplexing. It's easy to get into the routine of life and find yourself wandering without significance. God has you here for a reason, but maybe you're not sure what the reason is. You see everyone else walking in their purposes and callings, but you long to know what yours is. Being unsure about your purpose can leave you feeling lost or as if there is a void in your life that must be filled. It can feel like everyone else is being used by God and that your existence doesn't have much worth or essence. Many people walk through life with this sense of uncertainty hanging over them. They're not sure what they're supposed to do or where they're supposed to do it. Understanding why you are here is a lot simpler than we make it out to be. Actually, there's no secret formula to finding your purpose. No test will reveal your purpose.

As you're living life, functioning in church ministries, following your dreams and passions, your purpose will be revealed. It's just that simple. Oftentimes, people want their purpose revealed before they step up and do anything. They wait and wait and wait without making a move. In their waiting, they're frustrated and fatigued. I've seen people sit comfortably idle for ten years and wonder, "What's my purpose?" Perhaps, you're one of those people. Finding your purpose requires action. But rather than sitting and waiting, get up and do. Rehearsing things in your head won't work and will only lead to a deeper lack of understanding and stagnation. Knowing why you are here requires action on your part. Prayerful action that is. Before you take on any endeavor, pray about it and ask for God's guidance. Then do it. If it's not where you're supposed to be, God will reveal that to you and redirect your steps.

A few years ago, I joined a mega church. I knew absolutely no one there. I had a feeling, however, that my purpose was within this new ministry. It just felt right; it felt comfortable. After being there a few short months, I volunteered with the Youth Ministry because that's where I served at my prior church. I loved Youth Ministry, so I just jumped right in. I didn't wait for a specific call or spend a lot of time thinking about it; I just went for it. Simultaneously, I started attending the Women's class on Sunday mornings. This group was empowering, engaging, and I loved fellowshipping with the women. So on Wednesdays, I served with the youth, and Sundays I fellowshipped with the women.

Shortly after, I felt unrest working with the youth and like God was transitioning me. So I devoted more time to connecting with women. Unbeknownst to me, God was unveiling a new purpose and a year later, I became a teacher and leader in the

Women's class. I didn't know anyone there before joining the church, but because I went there and started moving, the purpose for which I'd been sent was revealed. The only way you're going to know why you are here is to start moving. You may have to try out several different options, but you'll know when you have found the perfect fit. You'll operate in it, and it'll flow easily. You'll enjoy doing it and won't have to be coerced into it.

If for some reason, you're still looking for a formula, Deuteronomy 10:12–13 gives you clear instructions on what you should be doing, "And now, Israel, what does the Lord your God require of you, but to fear the Lord your God, to walk in all His ways and to love Him, to serve the Lord your God with all your heart and with all your soul and to keep the commandments of the Lord and His statutes which I command you today for your good?" It's that simple. We are all here to 1) fear the Lord; 2) walk in His ways and love Him; 3) serve the Lord with all our hearts; and 4) keep His commandments. Do this with all of your heart, and you will fulfill what God requires of all of his children.

For Such a Time as This

Through a series of God-ordained events, Esther found herself in the palace of King Ahasuerus. She didn't come from royalty, nor was she from a family with status, but this young woman was favored by God. Of all of the young beautiful virgins in the provinces of the kingdom, the king specifically chose Esther to be his queen. She pleased the king with her beauty, sweet spirit, and personality. She did not compel him to find favor in her, yet she carried out the duties given to her and the other young ladies to secure the position of queen.

A displaced orphan, Esther was raised by her uncle, Mordecai. His prompting led Esther to eventually become queen, and it was also his prompting that kept her from revealing her Jewish race or nationality to anyone else until the time was right. Great prejudice existed at the time, and Mordecai warned Esther that it was not wise to reveal her heritage within the palace. She honored him and also remained in contact with him, regularly checking on his well-being. She never forgot where she came from, though she was now exposed to wealth and riches behind the palace doors.

However, there was unrest outside the palace doors. When she heard of the plot to kill her people, the Jews, Esther was devastated and didn't know what direction to take. Her uncle sent word to her to petition the king on behalf of her people. The problem was that she hadn't seen the king in thirty days. Customarily, the king would not accept anyone in his presence unless he had summoned them. Nevertheless, her purpose and reason for being the queen were much larger than a title, beauty, and wealth which afforded her position. She had a purpose.

While she pondered her next move, Mordecai asked her "Who knows but that you have come to your royal position for such a time as this?" (Esth. 4:14). Esther didn't go looking for purpose or even ask why she was chosen to be the queen; instead, she respectfully obeyed everything she was told to do. It was at this moment that God eventually revealed her specific calling: to save her people from annihilation. He made her the queen to fulfill His ultimate purpose.

Esther would have to go to the king on behalf of her people. Action was now needed for her to truly walk in her purpose. Nevertheless, before she proceeded, she fasted and prayed for direction and guidance. She was sure that God ordained the task that she was embarking on. So with prayer and caution, Esther went before King Ahasuerus and explained to him the evil plot that had been devised. As a result of her obedience to her assignment, this queen was able to save her people from death. Her purpose was revealed because of her willingness to trust for such a time as this.

A Perfect Fit

Going back to Cinderella. In the end, the glass slipper fit only one person's foot—Cinderella's—for it had been designed and made just for her. This was more than just a shoe, however. Contained in it were her hurts, haters, and history. Everything she had experienced positioned her for the moment that she would slip her foot into the glass shoe, a perfect fit. The shoe was uniquely hers. And your purpose is uniquely yours. Your story may resemble someone else's, but there's only one you. Accept that everyone isn't going to be pleased with your purpose. Jesus's purpose was to come to earth and save people, and do you know that today people are still not pleased with His purpose? Your purpose isn't given to you for you to please people; your aim is to please God. As long as you please God, your purpose will promote you. It will place you before great men and women. David wrote that "He will prepare a table for you even in the presence of your enemies" (Ps. 23:5). Don't worry about others. Keep pursuing your passions, for they will lead you to your purpose.

Lesson Seven
Live to the Fullest

My mission in life is not merely to survive, but to thrive;
and to do so with some passion, some compassion,
some humor and some style.

Maya Angelou

I have come that they may have life, and have it to the full.

John 10:10b

A lesson I had to learn is to live life to the fullest.

Life is meant to be enjoyed and lived. We are supposed to have full and prosperous lives. Of course, we will experience pain and disappointments, setbacks and frustrations, but even in the midst of those realities, we can still live an abundant life!

By nature, I'm a serious person. I'm all business, then more business, and then I'll play later down the road. I've been like that all of my life. I believe I inherited it from my dad. Growing up, he was a serious businessman. Lately, however, I'm learning to enjoy life's journey. To cherish every single moment and season because I will never be here again. This moment, once it's passed, will never return. The same is for you, too. Whatever season you're in, you'll never be there again. So cherish this moment. Soak it all in. Bask in the present, because it's a gift.

A few years ago, I traveled to Thailand with a friend. The flight lasted a grueling twenty-two hours. Most people despise long flights, but I don't really mind the trips because I enjoy traveling and seeing the world. However, on the way to our amazing vacation, we had a ten-hour layover in China. Can you imagine being confined in an airport for ten hours? We didn't know what to do with ourselves. We were focused on getting to Thailand, so we sat in the airport, ate, people watched, tried to nap, and then ate again before boarding the flight for the final leg to our destination.

When we arrived in Thailand, we met up with a group of people in our tour group who had also traveled from the States. After visiting and getting to know a few of them, we learned that some people had a much more enjoyable journey on their way to Thailand. Before leaving home, they made plans to take advantage of the ten-hour layover. When they arrived in China, they left the airport, went on a scheduled tour, and enjoyed the sights and sounds of the city. My friend and I were shocked that we didn't think to embrace the journey on the way to our destination. It didn't even cross our minds. We dreaded the layover, complained about how long we were going to sit in the airport, and lamented how this segment made the trip so much longer. What if we'd enjoyed the journey along the way? What if we'd celebrated the moment? We would have had an even greater story to tell.

We enjoyed Thailand, and on our way back home, we stopped in China again for yet another long layover. This time, though, we were better prepared for the predestined delay. We left the airport and intentionally cherished the moment at the Great Wall of China, one of the Seven Wonders of the World. It was breathtaking and amazing to see this gigantic wall that I'd only heard about in history class. I almost missed out on a priceless experience, being so focused on the destination rather than enjoying the journey. Now I have another country to add to my repertoire simply because I cherished the moment.

Living a full life means living a contented life. Paul reminds us to be content in every circumstance (Phil. 4:11). When your focus shifts from your problems to gratitude for the life you're blessed to live, then you begin to live to the fullest. A full life is peace of mind, stability, serenity, and tranquility. It's a life full of "love, joy, peace, patience, kindness, goodness, faithfulness, gentleness and self-control" (Gal. 5:22–23). There is no cost to live this type of life, but there are many rewards.

Remove the Limits

Do you realize that the only thing that can stop you from living a full, abundant life, is you? You can keep yourself from the life you've dreamed of. You can block the life God planned for you. You may have determined that time, money, resources, education, marital status, children, and the list goes on are why you can't live a full life. But those are all excuses keeping you from where you know you should be. You say you don't have much time. Well then, allocate your time more efficiently.

I often think of how much Oprah and Beyoncé have accomplished. They have the same twenty-four hours in their days that I have. To take it a step further, my family is from Mississippi, as is Oprah, and I was born in Houston, TX, like Beyoncé. I share roots with both of my "sheroes" of success. If they were able to reach their levels of success, then what's stopping me from going after everything God has placed on my heart? What's stopping you? If it's money, resources, or education, you can change that. There is money to be made; go make it. Resources are available; go find them. Schools will always be open; attend and learn. Maybe it's your family who is trying to stop you. Don't let them. Share your dreams and visions with them, show them the life you desire to live, and then go for it! If you do nothing now, nothing will change. But if you start taking steps toward your full life now, your life will be different later. Several small steps in the right direction will guarantee to land you at your destination. It's totally up to you!

She Rises Above Them All

Many women are depicted in the Bible, but the Proverbs 31 woman rises above them all. She represents a woman who lives life to the fullest and doesn't allow societal norms, family life, and daily responsibilities to keep her from the life God handcrafted for her. I love that this woman is unnamed because we all can insert our names into the account.

Who can find a virtuous wife? For her worth *is* far above rubies.
The heart of her husband safely trusts her; So, he will have no lack of gain.
Constance does him good and not evil. All the days of her life.
Constance seeks wool and flax, and willingly works with her hands.
Constance is like the merchant ships,
Constance brings her food from afar.
Constance also rises while it is yet night, and provides food for her household, and a portion for her maidservants.
Constance considers a field and buys it; from her profits, she plants a vineyard. She girds herself with strength and strengthens her arms.
Constance perceives that her merchandise *is* good, and her lamp does not go out by night.
Constance stretches out her hands to the distaff, and her hand holds the spindle.
Constance extends her hand to the poor, yes, she reaches out her hands to the needy.
Constance is not afraid of snow for her household, for all her household *is* clothed with scarlet.
Constance makes tapestry for herself; her clothing is fine linen and purple.
Constance's husband is known in the gates when he sits

among the elders of the land.

Constance makes linen garments and sells them, and supplies sashes for the merchants.

Strength and honor *are* her clothing;

Constance shall rejoice in time to come.

Constance opens her mouth with wisdom, and on her tongue *is* the law of kindness.

Constance watches over the ways of her household, and does not eat the bread of idleness.

Constance's children rise up and call her blessed; her husband also, and he praises her:

"Many daughters have done well, but *Constance* excel(s) them all."

Charm is deceitful and beauty is passing, but a woman who fears the Lord, she shall be praised.

Give her of the fruit of her hands, and let her own works praise her in the gates.

When you insert your name in this passage, it comes alive. The words on the pages go from black-and-white to bright, vivid colors. While you may not do every single thing this virtuous woman does, you can exemplify her characteristics of strength, excellence, and love. Her model of a full life is encouragement for us to excel in every area of our lives: relationships, careers, homes, and communities. We, too, can be like this godly woman.

Your Destiny May Look Different

Looking at the list the Proverbs 31 woman performed, or the activities Oprah and Beyoncé continue to be involved with, can seem overwhelming. Their lives aren't intended to convict or overwhelm us. However, God shows us the journeys of others to encourage us to dream our own destinies. Many people who have dreams have been inspired by someone else's journey or path. Though you may get your inspiration from someone else, it won't be exactly like theirs. It will be your own. Your destiny may look different from anyone else's, but that does not mean it's not what you're supposed to be doing. We are all unique. God handcrafted each of us, including our destinies.

There is so much that God desires to accomplish. He needs each of us operating in our specific destinies to achieve His plan. Your personality, your flavor, your twist, or your approach is essential to success. The world needs what you have to give in the manner you have to give it. We've already seen how someone else has done what you have set out to do, but God wants you to do it your way, proud and unashamed.

Even before Jesus left His disciples to go back to heaven, He told them that "Greater works than these will you do" (John 14:12). Even though they were Christ followers, their ultimate destinies would be different from the life Jesus lived. He expected them to live their lives in a way that honored Him but was still different, actually greater than His. So if Jesus expects our lives to be different from His, then surely it should be different from others we come in contact with. Though people share similarities while pursuing their destinies, we cannot ignore the distinct differences that make their lives unique. Don't try to be a carbon copy of someone else. Be the original you that God created, and watch what God does in your life.

As you journey through life, your destiny will look different in each place you find yourself. Glean from your experiences because they're building your unique journey. These are essential opportunities God provides to cultivate and refine you into who He is calling you to be.

Not only will experiences help mold your destiny, but also education and reading will help broaden your perspective. Knowledge can reroute your destiny and even completely change your course. Commit to being a lifelong student who desires wisdom, knowledge, and understanding. A wealth of knowledge is waiting for you to possess. Let it catapult you into your destiny. The sky's the limit.

Pursue Your Passions

Whatever you're dreaming, whatever you're desiring, pursue those passions. We tend to pursue what will bring us the most pleasure. So what truly makes you happy? Life is too short not to do what you love to do and are called to do. God placed your passions in your heart. He wants you to pursue them because He knows that when you pursue those longings in your heart, you will experience a fulfilling life. Christians should be the happiest, most fulfilled people on earth. We possess joy unspeakable and peace that surpasses understanding. We are blessed in the city and fields. We are called to live abundant lives.

Are you passionate about cooking? Are you passionate about writing? Are you passionate about helping others? Are you passionate about encouraging? Are you passionate about speaking? Whatever your passion, find opportunities to use and pursue them. Remember, there are no limits. Cook for families in need. Write articles for your local newspaper. Volunteer at nursing homes. Encourage young people in your family. Share your experiences with other women. Seize every opportunity to go after your passions relentlessly! You deserve it. The world deserves it.

And as a caterpillar transitions into a beautiful butterfly, so you will experience your own metamorphosis and LIVE the life God planned for you.

ACKNOWLEDGMENTS

To my heavenly Father! Thank you for patiently waiting for me to complete the assignment You'd given me a few years ago. You are so gracious, faithful, and sovereign.

To my parents, Joseph and Connie Darby. I truly believe God hand-picked you for me. I appreciate your never-ending support for everything my confident mind sets out to do. You are wonderful parents, and I'm so grateful for all you do for me.

To my Sisters, Cereece and Courtlyne. I am so proud to be your sister. You two are amazing and I love you dearly.

To DeNisha Dorian. There are no words to convey my gratitude. This is our book. Thank you for being a true friend.

To Mrs. Margene Meins, my 4th grade teacher at Lexington Creek Elementary. Thank you for encouraging my mom to enroll me in writing classes at such a young age. I remember those evenings spent at Wharton Junior learning how to be a better writer. I'm forever grateful to you for planting the seed in me.

To my Village. That's a lot of you!! To extended family, friends, church members, mentors, colleagues, and anyone with whom I have relationship. I love you all!

To all of my *Lessons*. You made me who I am today. Thank you.

ABOUT THE AUTHOR

Constance Danielle Darby is a confident woman from Houston, TX who is full of purpose and passion. It's no coincidence that she personifies the true meaning of her name. She is a Woman of God, author, and motivator. Constance knows who she is, whose she is, and is unashamedly living the life God orchestrated for her.

Constance is the first of three daughters to Joseph and Connie Darby. At an early age, she exemplified a love for God and would spend countless hours at her home church, Riceville Mt. Olive Baptist, staying with her aunt or other church members even when her parents were not there. Ministry became her passion. Constance has ministered in several settings from church services to conferences and retreats to school environments. She is willing to share the Word to whoever, whenever.

Constance has always been driven by empowering others. She formed Girlfriends Bible Study in 2014 a ministry where she connects with girlfriends to share the Word of God and grow together. She has also been a successful entrepreneur empowering others to reach their personal goals. Constance always shares that in order to be where you want to be in life, you have to set goals along the way. She is also a lead teacher in her church's Women's Group. She is honored to minister God's Word to women of all generations, cultures and walks of life.

Constance enjoys reading, watching movies, and traveling the world. She embraces opportunities to visit one of God's creations, and will forever cherish her "trip of a lifetime" to Israel. Constance loves God and is always willing to work for Him. She lives her life based on 1 Corinthians 15:58, which says "Therefore, my beloved brethren, be ye steadfast, unmovable, always abounding in the work of the Lord, forasmuch as ye know that your labor is not in vain in the Lord."

27045301R00061

Made in the USA
Columbia, SC
18 September 2018